FIBONACCI TRADING

SUPPORT AND RESISTANCE, SUPPLY AND DEMAND,STRATEGY YOU NEED TO KNOW FOR PROFIT

Harold Keith

TABLE OF CONTENT

INTRODUCTION

Fibonacci Retracement is an uncommonly intriguing marker to look at. It is an overlay marker which is used to find expected help and resistance levels. The marker plots different even lines that exhibit possible S/R levels

The not entirely set in stone considering Fibonacci numbers. To get a handle on the marker and worth its beginning stage, we will cover all of the subjects right in light of what are Fibonacci numbers to how the pointer can be used to construct your possibilities while exchanging

The Fibonacci retracement begins from the Fibonacci progression, which elements sponsorship and obstacle levels by characterizing level limits on an expense frame. The retracement levels are set at results of 1.618 or the splendid extent. For example, the important retracement level is at 23.6%, followed continually level at 38.2%, the third at 61.8%, and the fourth at 78.6%. Consequently, when there is significant solid areas for an or downtrend, the expense, generally speaking, recollects at any of these levels

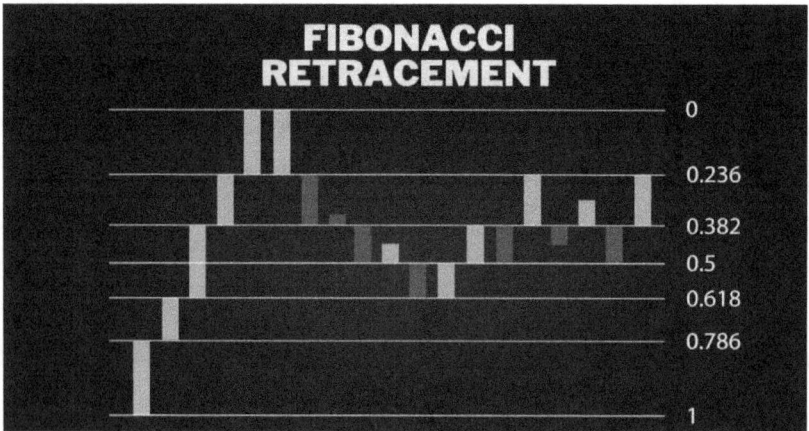

The Fibonacci retracements are extensively used to choose cost levels for inspirations and pullbacks in an upswing or a downtrend. For example, in an upswing, the expense often makes little pullbacks and a while later again floats upwards.

CHAPTER ONE

INTRODUCTION TO FIBONACCI VS ANY OTHER INDICATOR

Moving typical example following system versus Fibonacci exchanging structure. The basic vendor assembles his choices as for an example following technique. He is using two 9-and 21-period direct moving midpoints. Right when the 9 Mom crosses the 21 Mom, a buy signal is created. Right when 9 Mom crosses back under 21 Mom, the opportunity has arrived to leave the exchange. Here is a representation of a moving common example following procedure.

On account of the fast expense improvement and the late Mom cross, the entry point was to some degree late. The leave signal appeared preposterously late. Moreover, if the expense gives significant retracement, you will be out of trade no matter what the expense push toward you. In this model, the significant retracement happens.

The Fibonacci technique is being used by the other representative. He decides to trade swing, plots the Fibonacci retracement levels, and searches for an section signal at the level of retracement. Enter the plan when the sign appears. To choose when to end the trade, he in like manner draws the Fibonacci expansions level.

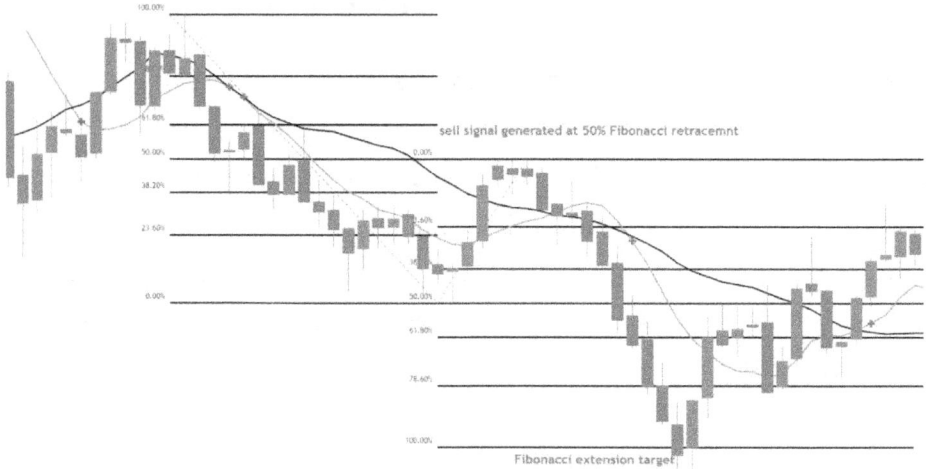

While the moving common example follows the structure, the fundamental dealer, decided to enter the trade. To make an increase, it was very late. Take a gander at the resulting vendor (Fibonacci). See that he made his entry and leave decisions quite a while before the essential vendor did. He extended his advantage on a comparable chart and shut it while the hidden intermediary was meanwhile trusting that the example will continue.

What Are the Different Fibonacci Exchanging Devices and How to Apply Them?

The Fibonacci gadgets are used to perceive segments, backing and resistance, targets, and exits. These two are the most extensively used:
- ☐Fibonacci retracement
- ☐Fibonacci development

What is a Fibonacci Retracement and how to utilize it?

The fundamental norm of the Fibonacci retracement trading method. According to the speculation, the expense will backtrack following starting a new prevailing fashion making a beeline for happening in the example's course. Hence, to conclude the accompanying conceivable assistance and resistance levels, we use the Fibonacci instrument.

The retracement level predicts the main level at which retracement is possible. These retracement levels offer agents a remarkable chance to open new trades the example's going.

- The Fibonacci retracement levels are 23.6%, 38.2%, 50%,61.8%, 78.6%, and 100 percent.

Next conceivable help levels are stamped if the stock climbs

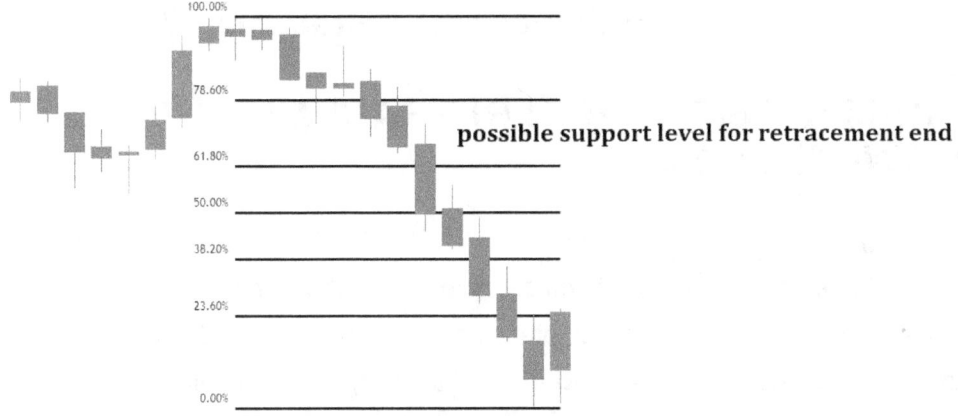

Basic Fibonacci Trading Strategy

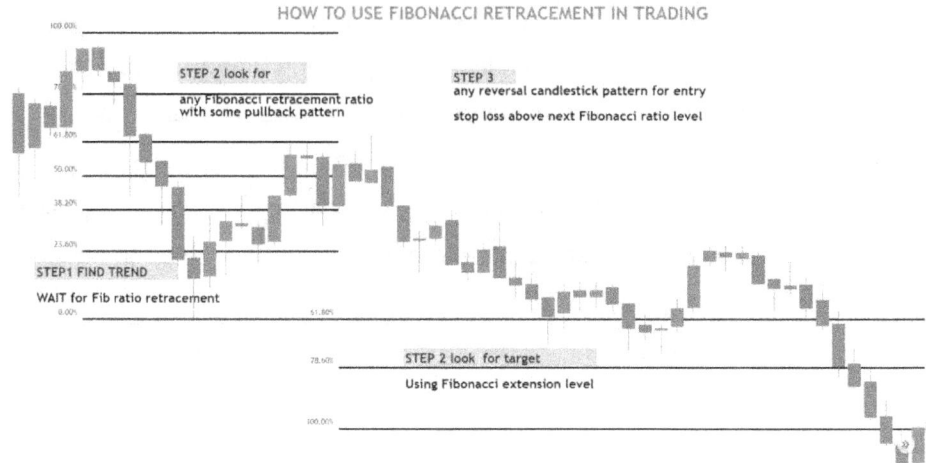

How to draw Fibonacci Retracement?

EXAMPLE FIBONACCI RETRACEMENT IN A DOWNTREND

You ought to find the most recent critical Swing Ups and Swing Downs to conclude these Fibonacci retracement levels. Find the new swing HIGH (early phase) and late swing LOW (completing point). then, joint the 2 lines. Drag the pointer to the most recent Swing LOW to swing HIGH and find all retracement level

- ☐0.618 is the splendid retracement level

- ☐.0.5 to .618 is the devil retracement level in the example

- Use the Fibonacci instrument close by the transformation factor for segments.

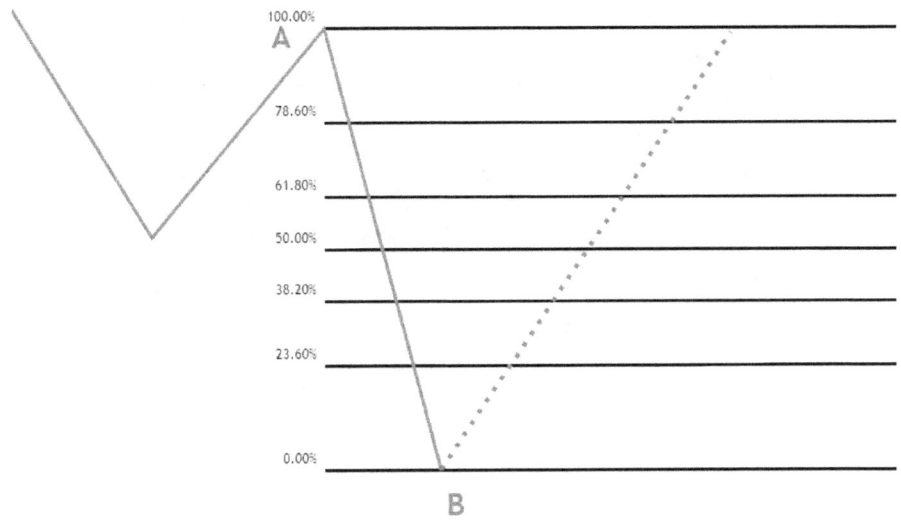

Above outline cost follow 61.8% level. THE Beneath Graph is the continuation of the above diagram. yet, backtrack half

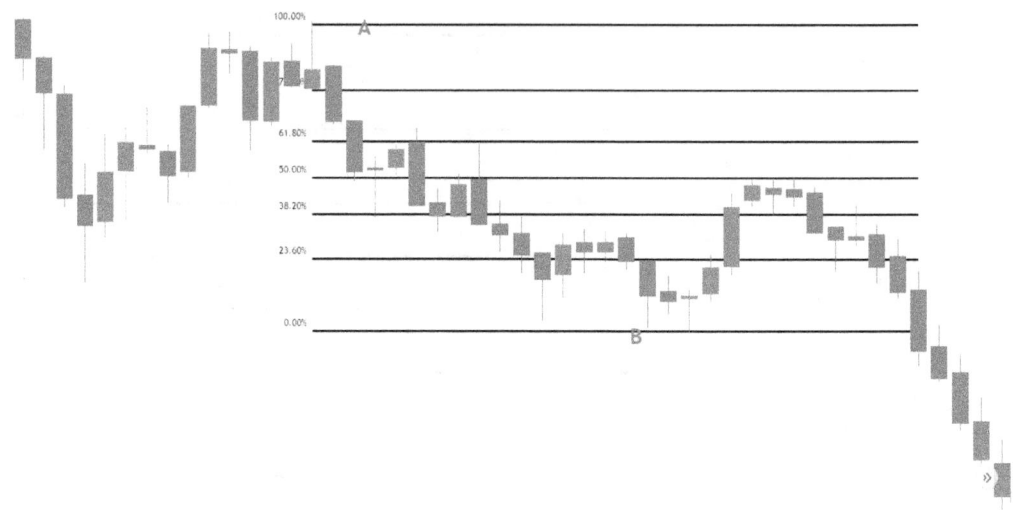

Again, the below chart is the continuation of the above chart and retraces 78.6%

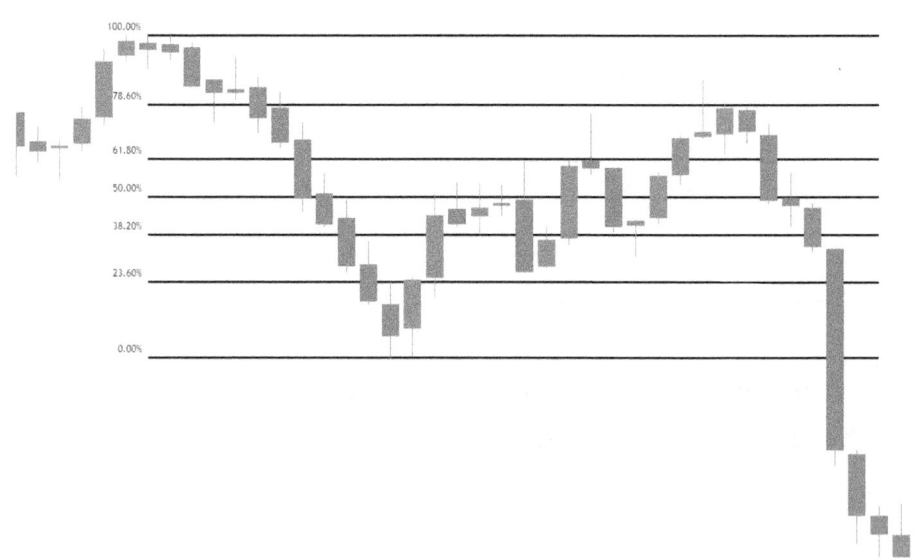

CHAPTER TWO

WHAT IS THE FIBONACCI EXTENSION AND HOW TO USE IT

How to draw Fibonacci Extensions

Fibonacci Improvement relies upon three core interests. Here are the step for a downtrend

Stage 1 - Recognize the course of the market: downtrend. To draw in it we really want to recognize the inspiration swing (An and B centers) and retracement end (C point).

Stage 2 - Attach the Fibonacci expansion gadget on the swing high and drag it aside, the whole way to the swing low.

Stage 3 - As of now, drag again back to the retracement end (point C)

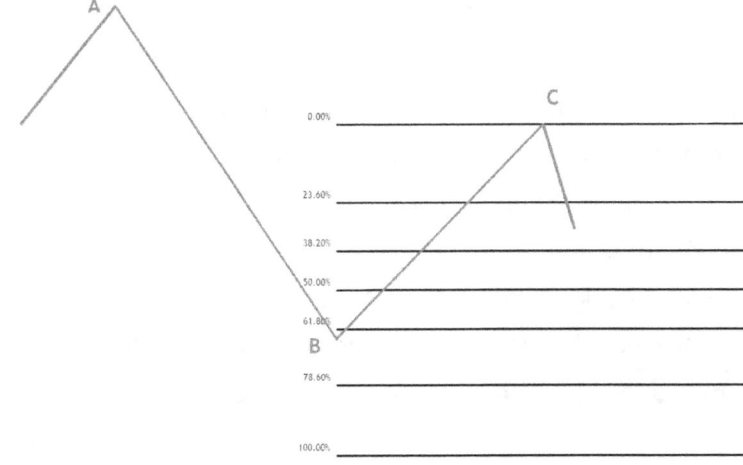

Why use Fibonacci Augmentations in Trading

Opening a trade is essentially less basic than closing it. Extension device for leave cost objective. Sellers can include Fibonacci developments as an instrument to set benefit targets or predict how far a market could rise when a retracement is done. Development levels are another probable region at an expense reversal.

Fibonacci expansion levels are extremely valuable in unwinding market reversals and probable street checks. Fundamentally, Fibonacci expansion levels are the essential concentrations from which the expense of an instrument could change.

The Fibonacci Retracement Gadget simplifies it to fan out increases by means of normally recognizing a couple of development levels where expenses can go around. Typical Fibonacci extension levels are 61.8%, 100%, 161.8%, 200%, and 261.8%.

To totally leave a trade or book a midway advantage, intermediaries ought to consent to explicit principles. They realize that there is a nice likelihood the improvement will arrive at a resolution or reprieve for quite a while.

Segment what is going on into three areas, which is the principal benefit booking framework vendors use. At 100% development, the underlying portion is quickly closed. You close the second part at the 161.8% extension accepting that the worth continues to advance toward the example. You let the third part increase before genuinely closing it using either a specific trigger or an extension level that is interesting.

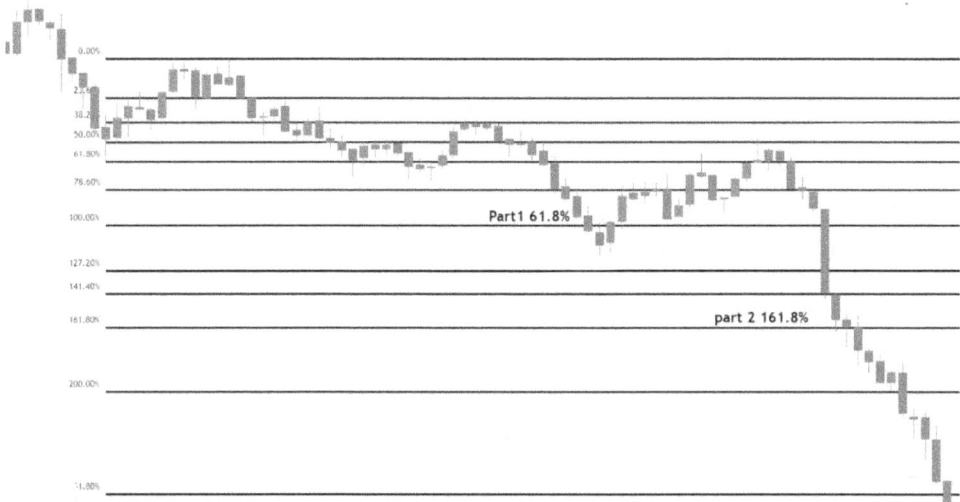

Contrast Between Fibonacci Retracement and Fibonacci Expansion

Fibonacci Retracement	Fibonacci Expansion
Shows how profundity of retracement after drive move.	Demonstrates where the cost might go pursuing a retracement in the direction
Measures Pullbacks Inside a Pattern. value revision or time remedy	Measures the pattern motivations waves toward the pattern
Give successful stop-misfortune levels and section orders for a pattern exchanging methodology.	Gives great take-benefit focuses in pattern exchanging and inversion focuses for pattern inversion strategies.
With different conjunctions, it tends to be successfully utilized as a	It tends to be applied to a

productive methodology.	methodology for taking benefits and may likewise demonstrate promising focuses for pattern inversions.
Fibonacci Numbers are inside the underlying pattern. (38.2%, 61.8%, half, and so on.)	Fibonacci Numbers are past the 100 percent Fibonacci level. (1.618%, 123.60%, and so forth.)

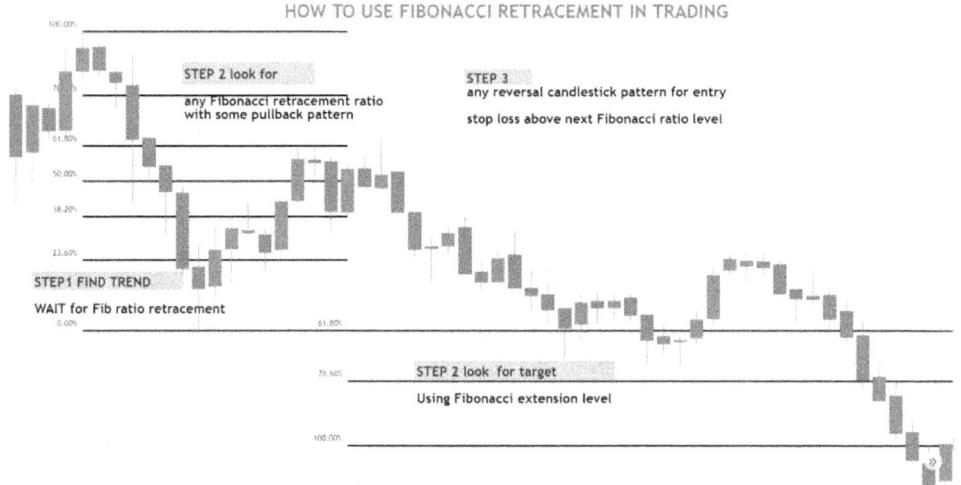

The Fibonacci method works best when the market is moving, which is the most compelling thing you should be know all about it. Right when the market is moving upward, the plan is to buy a retracement at a Fibonacci support level. Besides, when the market is declining, it is reasonable to sell a retracement at a Fibonacci hindrance level. Since Fibonacci retracement levels endeavor to foresee where the expense might be from now on, they are seen as a kind of specific pointer.

- □What Fibonacci retracement levels could it be really smart for me to use?
- □Should the expense contact the retracement levels?
- □What convergence component to check for more strong area?
- □How to take entry (powerful/moderate/safe area)?

- □Where to place stop hardship considering section?

- □Where to take entry?

What Fibonacci Retracement Levels Should I use

Since there are so many Fibonacci retracement levels, it is astoundingly perplexing all along. Fibonacci Retracements are not segment signals, they are target districts where an entry sign could occur. Trading basically considering the way that the expense has shown up at a Fibonacci retracement extent level is certainly not a shrewd framework. Another crossing point is normal before trades can be taken.

- In the event that u use Fibonacci Retracements level with different ideas affirming like pattern line, turn point, or any powerful help or opposition

Should the cost touch the retracement levels?

Since there are so many Fibonacci retracement levels, it is astoundingly perplexing all along. Fibonacci Retracements are not segment signals, they are target districts where an entry sign could occur. Trading basically considering the way that the expense has shown up at a Fibonacci retracement extent level is certainly not a shrewd framework. Another crossing point is normal before trades can be taken.

How to take passage?

In a general sense, 3 sorts of segment can be taken after a Fibonacci retracement.

- □Powerful area
- □Moderate section
- □Safe section

Which section is the best for you? It is your decision. It depends upon danger, prize, and probability.

Forceful section after profound retracement

This is the most hazardous segment yet a little disaster and high award plan. You will confront a little test subsequently for a possible more noteworthy return. Right when the expense close/shows up at the 61.8% retracement, you go long at this level or a bit above it.

- ☐Perceive the example and level of Fibonacci retracement level.
- ☐Look for the convergence factor
- ☐Keep it together for a reversal flame plan for area
- ☐Draw expansion lines for the possible goal level
- ☐Put stop disaster past late high in downtrend also past Fibonacci retracement level

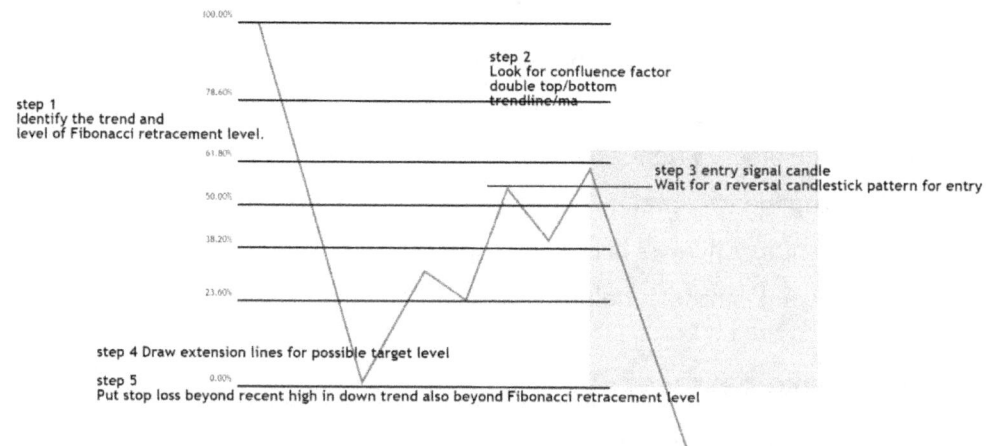

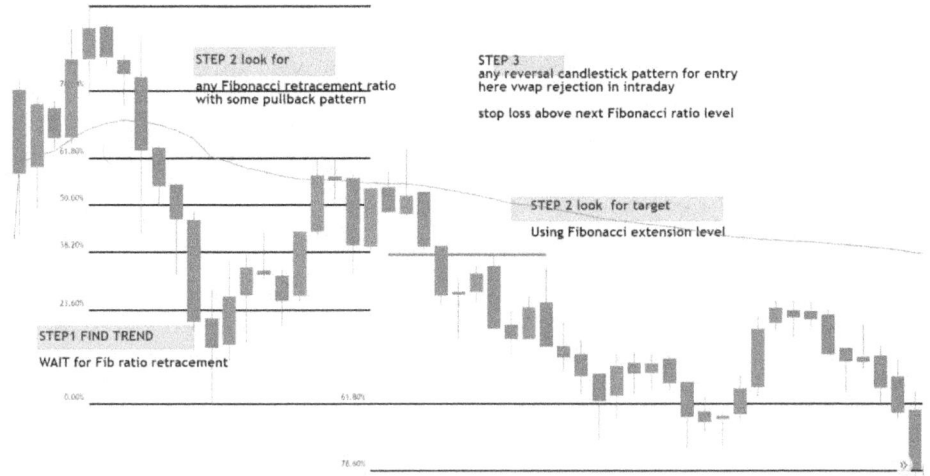

STEP 2 look for
any Fibonacci retracement ratio
with some pullback pattern

STEP 3
any reversal candlestick pattern for entry
here vwap rejection in intraday

stop loss above next Fibonacci ratio level

STEP 2 look for target
Using Fibonacci extension level

STEP1 FIND TREND

WAIT for Fib ratio retracement

Moderate Section

The moderate segment is the place where you delay and watch how the expense answers toward the retracement levels. Expecting that you see that 61.8% is probably the retracement which a return rapidly may occur from, you are ready to take a long position. Be that as it may, not by any stretch of the imagination like the strong area case, you hold on for another certification. Break of minor swing low in the negative area. confirmation signals are not commonly 100% right, yet in light of everything, you have a lower chance of dissatisfaction. The extent among danger and possible advantage is perfect. In this model, the representative reasoned that the sign will be close under help.

1.Recognize the example and level of Fibonacci retracement level.

2.Search for the crossroads factor

3.Sit tight for the break of minor assistance for section for a negative trade

4.Draw development lines for the possible goal level

5.Put stop disaster past late high in downtrend moreover past Fibonacci retracement level

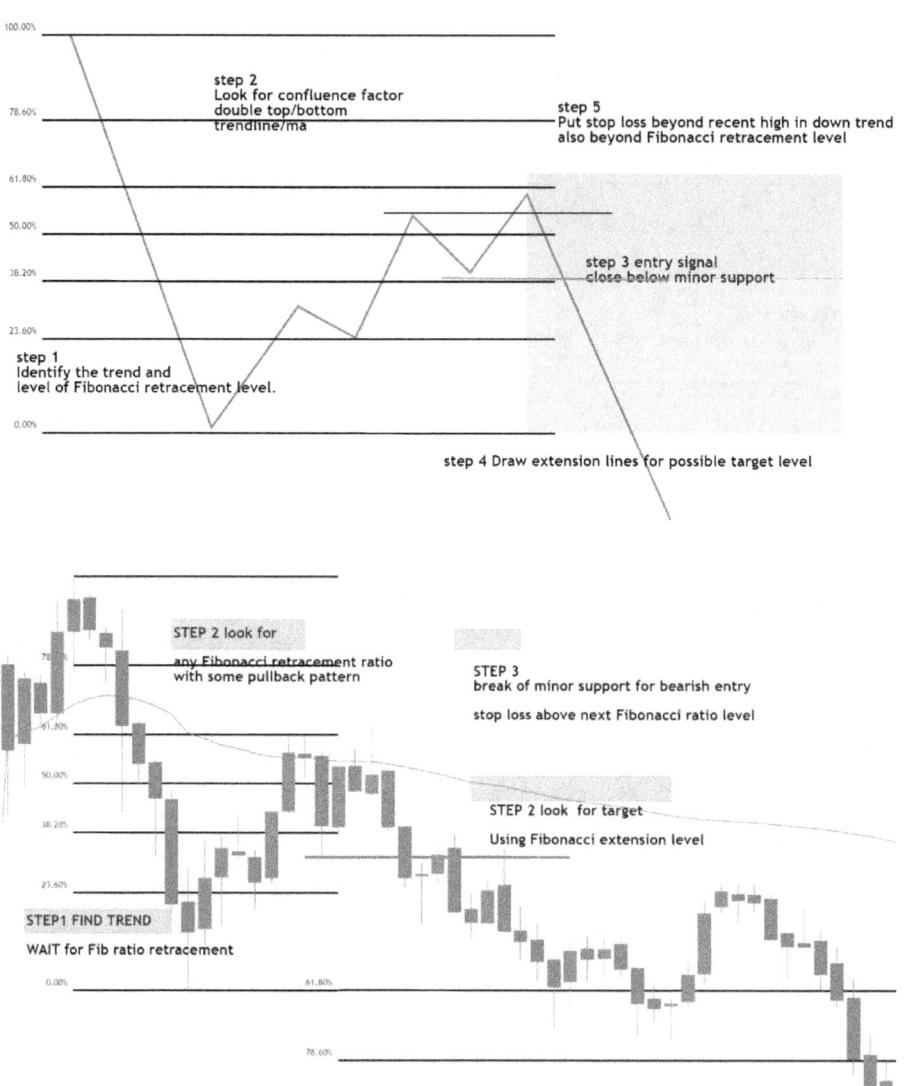

another illustration of both passage

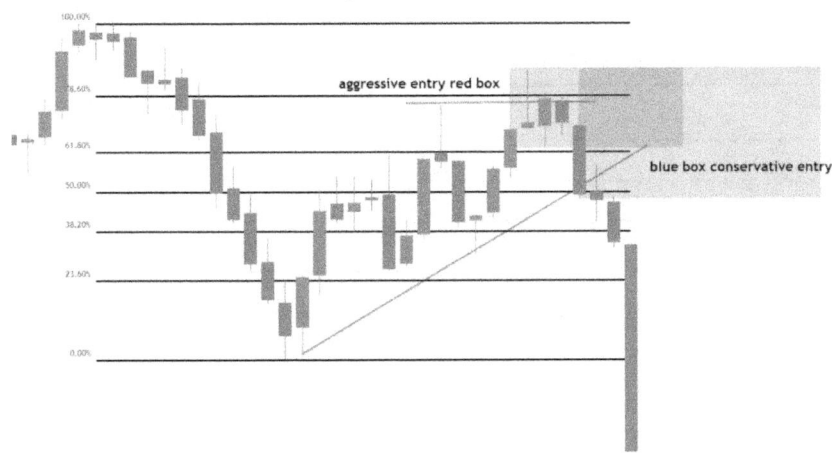

Safe Section

This way to deal with trading is the most reliable one differentiation with another 2 area methodologies, yet your possible advantage is the tiniest. The essential idea is to buy a breakout after an expense withdrawal.

On a fundamental level, it should appear to be in the picture under:

● ☐Perceive the example and level of Fibonacci retracement level.

● ☐Look for cost pressure before the breakout

● ☐Hold on for the break of help for segment for a negative trade

● ☐Draw expansion lines for the possible goal level

● ☐Put stop hardship past withdrawal high in a downtrend

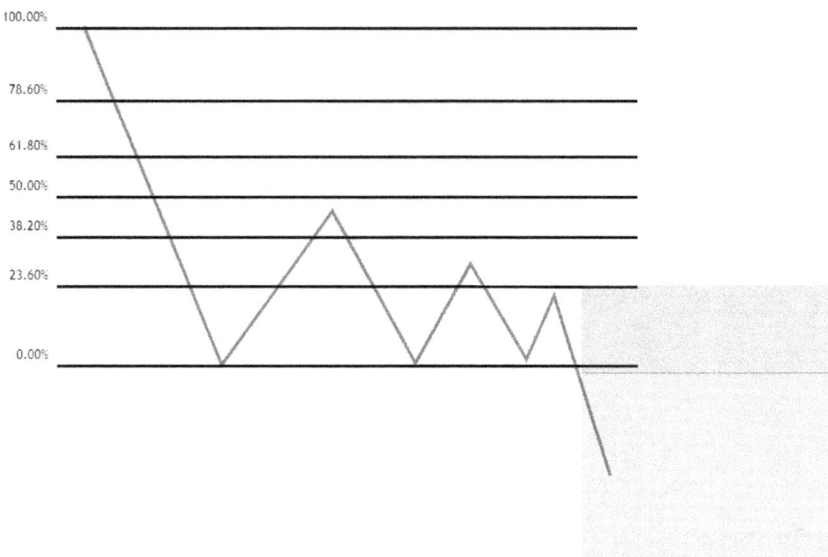

CHAPTER THREE

FIBONACCI TRADING STRATEGY USING CONFLUENCE FACTOR

Standards of Market Patterns

As you doubtlessly know cost movement has a confound structure

1. Developments with the example are assigned "main thrusts/expansions".

2. Developments against the example are assigned "amendment/retracement".

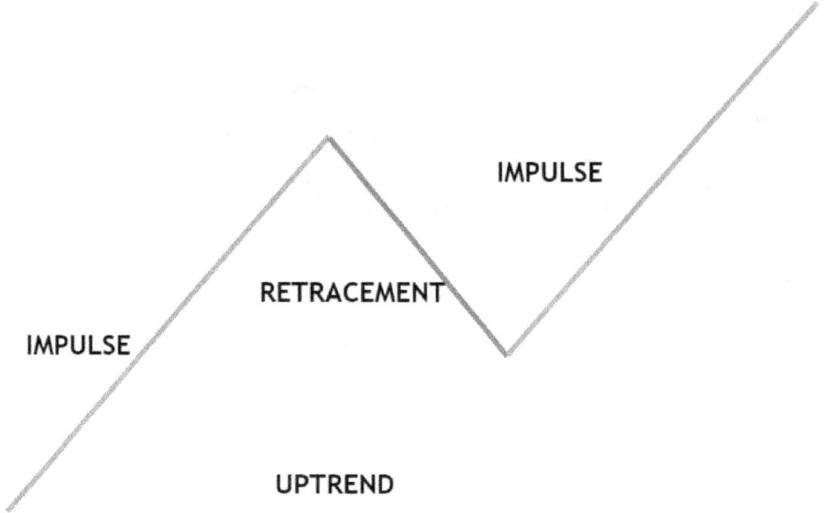

IMPULSE

RETRACEMENT

IMPULSE

UPTREND

Fibonacci Retracement

Following beginning a new prevailing fashion bearing, the expense will recollect before happening in the example's course. In like manner, we use the Fibonacci instrument to perceive the going with conceivable assistance and resistance levels. The best level at which retracement is likely going to happen is expected by the Fibonacci retracement level. Intermediaries have a fair opportunity to start new trades the example's going at these retracement levels.

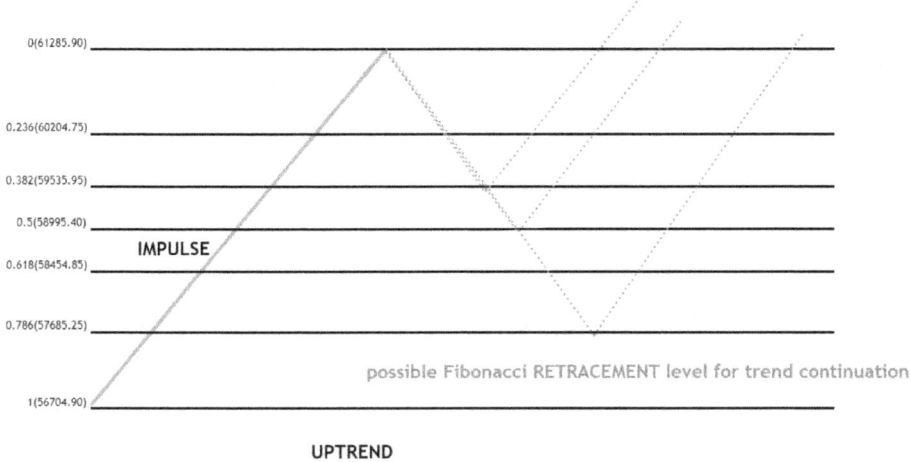

Fibonacci Expansion

Sellers can include Fibonacci developments as an instrument to set benefit targets or predict how far a market could rise when a retracement is done

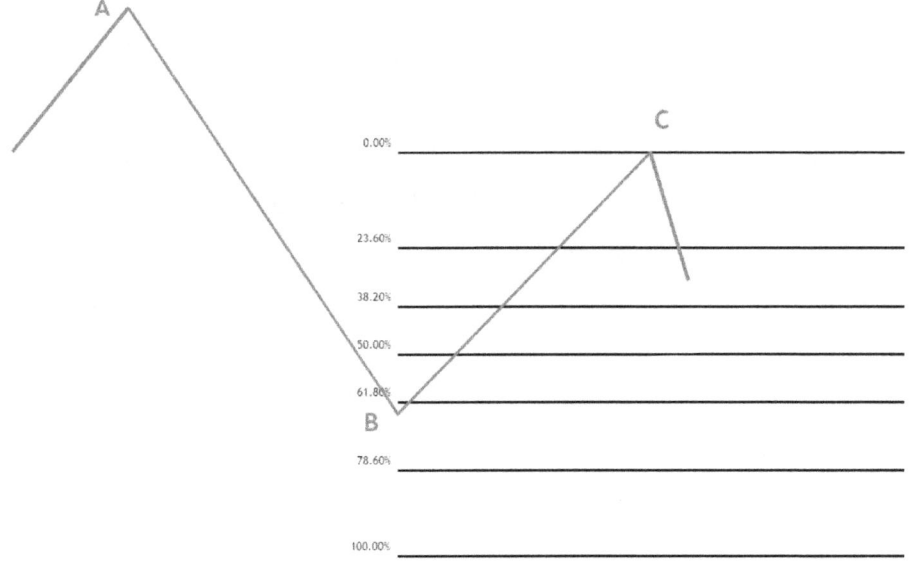

For what reason does Fibonacci Work?

A lot of representatives puts alerts at different Fibonacci retracement levels and quest for trade significant entryways at a prevalent expense

The expense movement seller furthermore looks for buy on dunks in spread out rises

☐Besides, some other pointer seller furthermore looks for entries like a pattern line. moving typical, etc

Every one of these juncture factors increment the likelihood of achievement

What is the Fibonacci retracement trading method?

Area of help in the rise and area of deterrent in the upswing. The chief idea behind the Fibonacci retracement trading strategy. states that right after beginning a new prevailing fashion heading, the expense will follow preceding happening in the example's bearing. Subsequently, we utilize the Fibonacci

mechanical assembly to recognize the going with likely assistance and hindrance levels. The best level at which retracement is most likely going to happen is expected by the retracement level. Dealers have a bewildering an entryway to start new trades the example's going at these retracement levels. The Fibonacci retracement levels are

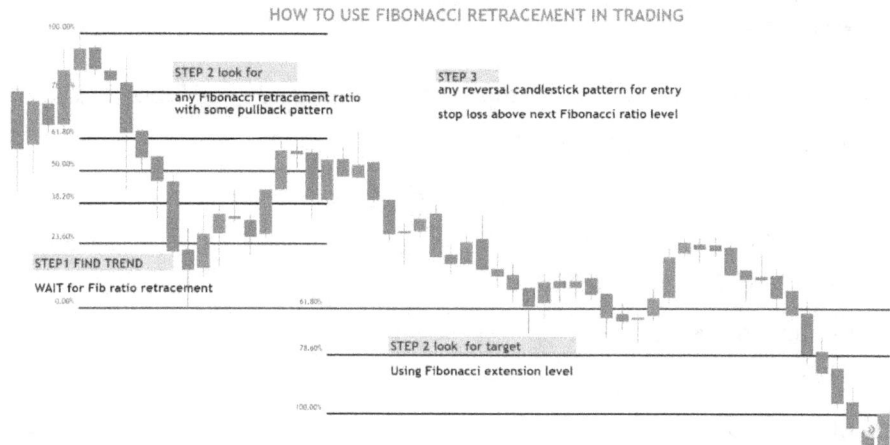

%, 38.2%, 50%,61.8%, 78.6%, and 100 percent.s

Next conceivable help levels are checked if the stock climb

What is the Area of Conversion?

Intersection implies tracking down different purposes behind taking an exchange. "Area of Conjunction" in exchanging alludes to a specific value zone or level when a few specialized examination devices and pointers join and propose a similar conceivable cost development. Intersection zones are viewed as more grounded degrees of help or opposition since the communication of a few boundaries adds more help to imminent cost activity. Many kinds of merchants take passage at a zone with a similar view which makes force in support of yourself.

The Fibonacci with conjunction factor exchanging technique includes consolidating the utilization of Fibonacci retracement levels with different boundaries to distinguish potential exchange open doors.

Tracking down Area of Conjunction in Fibonacci Exchanging Technique

Here are some juncture factors that can use alongside the Fibonacci retracement exchanging procedure

- Fibonacci retracement
- Even help and obstruction
- Organic market zone
- Trendline
- Moving normal
- Graph design

More the conversion more grounded the sign

1. **Fundamental things that search in exchanging Fibonacci conjunction** exchanging methodology
2. Pattern exchanging
3. Clear motivation move

The main pullback in a recently settled pattern

Fibonacci Trend line Intersection Exchanging Technique

The Fibonacci with trend line exchanging methodology includes consolidating the utilization of Fibonacci retracement levels with trend lines to recognize potential exchange open doors the monetary business sectors.

A trend line is a straight line that interfaces at least two costs and is utilized to distinguish the bearing of the latest thing in a market. With regards to the Fibonacci with trend line exchanging procedure, trend lines are utilized to affirm the course of the pattern and to decide the legitimacy of the Fibonacci retracement levels.

This is the way the technique works:

- **Recognize the pattern:** Quest for an instrument that is either rising (new records all around) or falling (worse high points and worse low points)

Draw a trend line: Define a boundary on the outline that interfaces at least two lows (for an upturn) or at least two highs (for a downtrend) to show the pattern. You can utilize the trend line as a degree of help or protection from help you to choose whether to trade.

- utilize the Fibonacci retracement instrument to figure out key degrees of retracement and search for the intersection of both trend lines with the Fibonacci retracement level

- **Recognize section and leave focuses:** Assuming that the cost is in an upturn or more the trend line, consider purchasing close to the help of the trend line. Consider selling at the trend line obstruction assuming the cost is underneath the trend line and the pattern is descending.

- Stop misfortune and target: - Put stop-misfortune orders beneath the trend line in an upswing or over the trend line in a slump to lessen risk. Also, consider utilizing benefit goals to augment benefits at predefined levels

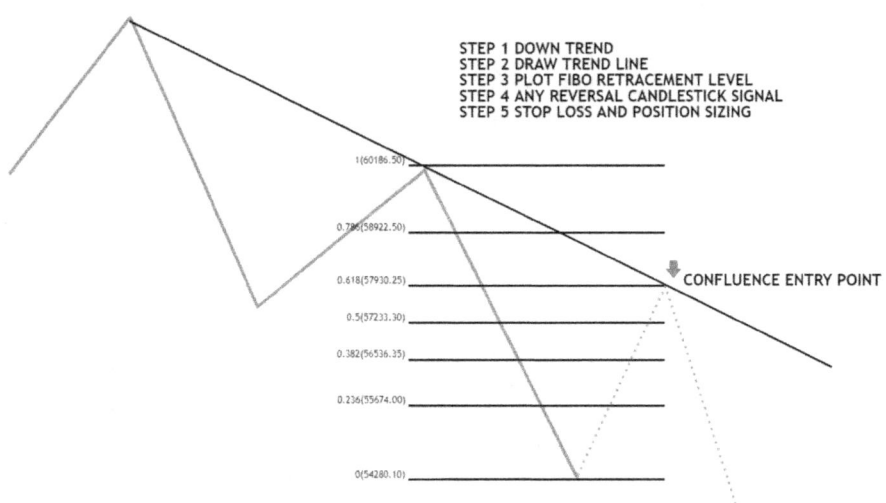

BELOW IS AN EXAMPLE OF A BANK NIFTY DAILY TIME FRAME

CHAPTER FOUR

FIBONACCI WITH SUPPORT AND RESISTANCE OR SUPPLY AND DEMAND ZONE CONFLUENCE TRADING STRATEGY

To find reasonable passage and leave valuable open doors, numerous dealers consolidate the conversion of Fibonacci retracement levels with support and resistance levels or supply and demand zone. To pinpoint spots where the cost might turn around, this technique consolidates Fibonacci retracement levels with huge support and resistance levels.

With this methodology, brokers search for intersection between significant support and resistance levels or market interest zone and Fibonacci retracement levels.

Here is a bit by bit guide on the most proficient method to utilize the intersection of Fibonacci retracement levels with help and opposition levels

- **The initial step is to distinguish an unmistakable pattern** on the lookout. This should be possible by taking a gander at the cost activity. implies there ought to be an unmistakable drive to move past help obstruction.
- **The subsequent step is to recognize key degrees of help and opposition or organic market zone in an unmistakable pattern**. This should be possible by searching for past price levels where the cost has breakout or turned around

- **The third step is to utilize the Fibonacci retracement instrument** to figure out the critical degree of retracement and search for the juncture of both help or obstruction with the Fibonacci retracement level
- **Recognize section and leave focuses**: On the off chance that the price is in an upturn consider purchasing close to the help of the trendline
- **Stop misfortune and target:** - ABOVE Passage SIGNAL HIGH IN DOWN Pattern.

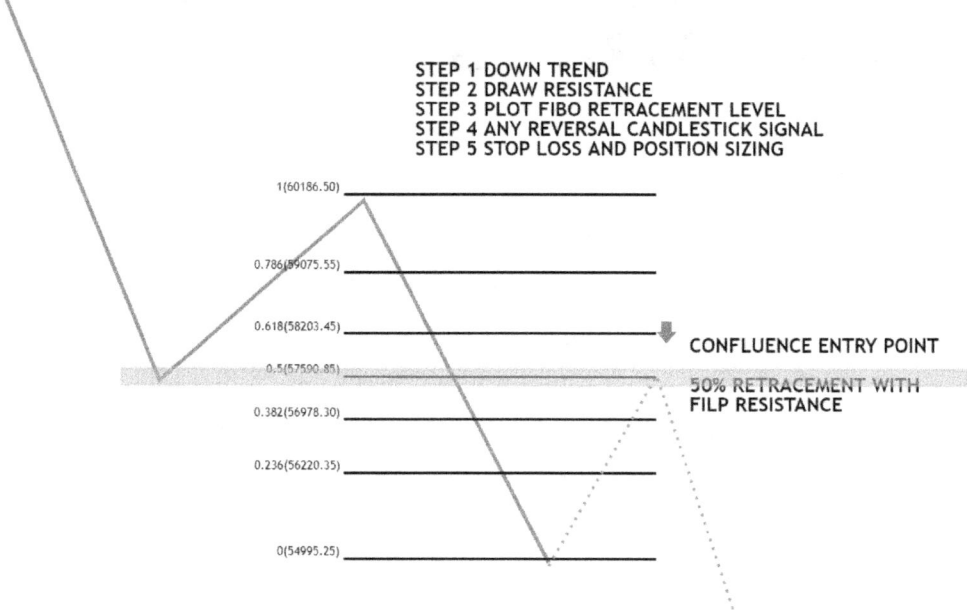

STEP 1 DOWN TREND
STEP 2 DRAW RESISTANCE
STEP 3 PLOT FIBO RETRACEMENT LEVEL
STEP 4 ANY REVERSAL CANDLESTICK SIGNAL
STEP 5 STOP LOSS AND POSITION SIZING

1(60186.50)

0.786(59075.55)

0.618(58203.45)

0.5(57590.85)

0.382(56978.30)

0.236(56220.35)

0(54995.25)

CONFLUENCE ENTRY POINT

50% RETRACEMENT WITH FILP RESISTANCE

Here is an illustration of a clever 2 hours time frame.505 Fibonacci retracement with flip opposition and afterward a downtrend proceeded

The following is the case of Fibonacci with an organic market zone and afterward a downtrend proceeded

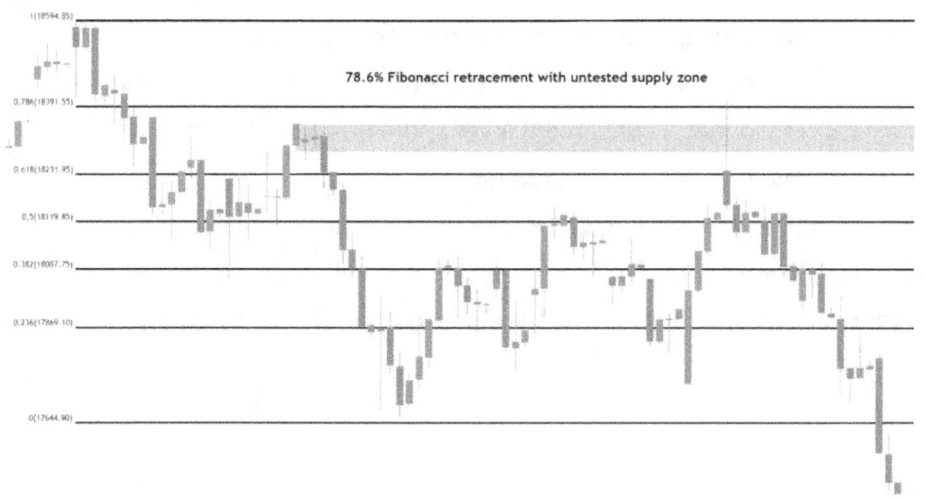

Fibonacci with Moving Average Confluence Trading Strategy:

Utilizing two notable pointers, the Fibonacci in addition to moving normal conjunction exchanging procedure can detect likely market patterns and inversions. Merchants search for conjunction between these two pointers to affirm their exchanging choices, and the methodology is well known among specialized experts for its precision in distinguishing potential exchanging amazing open doors.

1. Plot moving midpoints on your graph. Moving midpoints can assist with distinguishing the heading of the pattern and give likely areas of help and obstruction.
2. Utilize the Fibonacci retracement device to plot the Fibonacci levels between a high and depressed spot in the pattern.
3. search for conversion between the Fibonacci levels and the moving midpoints. In the event that a key moving normal lines up with a key Fibonacci retracement level, for example, the 61.8% or half retracement, this makes a more grounded area of help or opposition.
4. on the off chance that you find a conversion between the Fibonacci levels and the moving midpoints, the following stage is to pursue an exchange choice. For instance, assuming you track down a conjunction of help at the 61.8% Fibonacci retracement level and a 50-moving normal, you might choose to enter a long situation at that level

The following IS AN Illustration OF A Day to day Time period IN Clever. HERE THE conversion of 61.8% Fibonacci backtracks with flip help and 50 straightforward moving normal. then the cost go on with the pattern

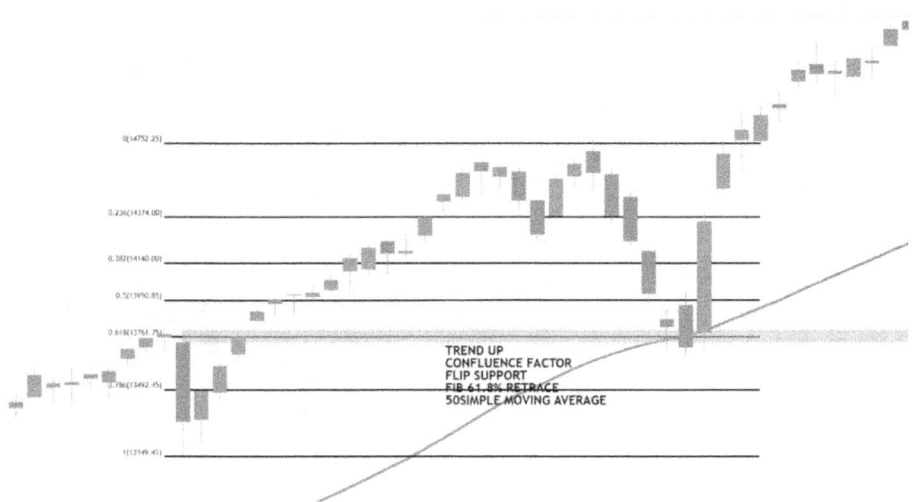

Fibonacci Exchanging Technique with Various Conjunction Elements

The Fibonacci with various juncture strategies utilizes different pointers to decide potential spots of help and opposition for section and exit on the lookout.

finding significant Fibonacci retracement levels and consolidating them with other juncture factors like moving midpoints, pattern lines, backing and obstruction levels, organic market zones, and outline designs. Merchants can get a more complete image of the market and possibly find more exact exchanging signals

Allow us to see one more illustration of the clever everyday time period and furthermore the expansion of the past diagram. Here the conjunction factor falling wedge, 100 straightforward moving normal with 61.8% Fibonacci follow likewise one can see a twofold base inversion

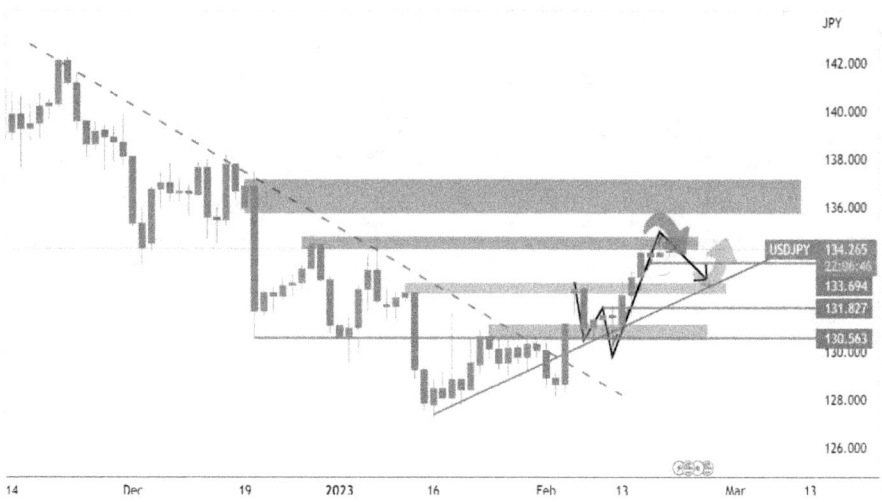